LEVEL 1

YOU READ · I READ

Elephants

Avery Elizabeth Hurt

NATIONAL GEOGRAPHIC

Washington, D.C.

How to Use This Book

Reading together is fun! When older and younger readers share the experience, it opens the door to new learning. As you read together, talk about what you learn.

This side is for a parent, older sibling, or older friend. Before reading each page, take a look at the words and pictures. Talk about what you see. Point out words that might be hard for the younger reader.

This side is for the younger reader.

As you read, look for the bolded words. Talk about them before you read. In each chapter, the bolded words are:
Chapter 1: describing words • Chapter 2: family names
Chapter 3: body parts • Chapter 4: survival words

At the end of each chapter, do the activity together.

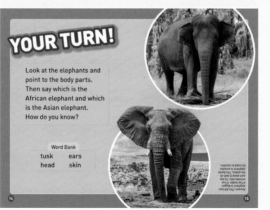

YOUR TURN!

Look at the elephants and point to the body parts. Then say which is the African elephant and which is the Asian elephant. How do you know?

Word Bank
tusk   ears
head   skin

Table of Contents

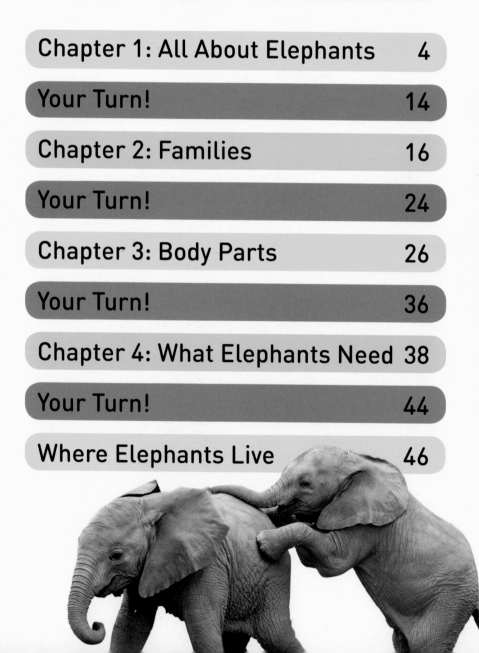

CHAPTER 1

All About Elephants

YOU READ An elephant is the biggest animal that lives on land. An adult elephant is much **bigger** than a truck, and can weigh up to 14,000 pounds!

I READ A baby elephant is **bigger** than an adult cheetah. It eats a lot and grows more every day.

YOU READ

There are two kinds of elephants, African elephants and Asian elephants. Although they have the **same** body parts, there are some differences.

Asian elephant

They are not the **same** size. African elephants are bigger.

African elephant

An Asian elephant has a rounder head, with a **large** bump on top. Not all Asian elephants have tusks, but all African elephants do.

tusk

I READ An elephant's tusk is like a **large** tooth. It grows as the elephant gets older.

YOU READ

African elephants live in deserts and plains where the temperature is very warm. They have big ears and **wrinkly** skin, with many lines and folds.

close-up picture of
elephant skin

It's hot here. **Wrinkly** skin and big ears help. They let heat leave the elephant's body.

YOU READ

Asian elephants live in **shady** jungles where there are plenty of trees and leaves. Their skin is smooth and their ears are small.

It isn't very hot in the **shady** jungle. Asian elephants don't need special body parts to stay cool.

YOUR TURN!

Look at the elephants and point to the body parts. Then say which is the African elephant and which is the Asian elephant.
How do you know?

Word Bank

tusk	ears
head	skin

Answer: The African elephant is bigger. It has tusks. It has wrinkly skin. Its big ears keep it cool on the plains. The Asian elephant is smaller. Its head is rounder.

CHAPTER 2

Families

YOU READ Elephants live in family groups called herds. The oldest **mother** is the leader, but there are other females in the herd, too.

Babies rest with their **mothers**. Other elephants make a circle around them. That keeps them safe.

YOU READ As the baby elephant grows, the **females** in the herd continue to take care of it. They protect the baby from danger.

A baby elephant can get stuck in mud. The **female** elephants pull the baby out.

YOU READ

A baby elephant is called a **calf**. It stays safe by holding on tightly to an older female's tail. The calf stays close to the herd so it doesn't get lost.

 The herd often travels in a line. A **calf** holds on to the tail in front.

When a **male** elephant gets older, he leaves the herd. Female calves stay with the herd.

 Some **male** elephants live alone. Some live with other males.

YOUR TURN!

Read the words under each line. Choose the word that finishes each sentence. Tell about elephant families.

female

calf

male

mother

The leader of the herd is

the oldest _____.
(mother/calf)

_____ elephants
(Female/Male)

sometimes live by themselves.

Older _____
(calf/female)

elephants help take care of

the _____.
(males/calves)

CHAPTER 3

Body Parts

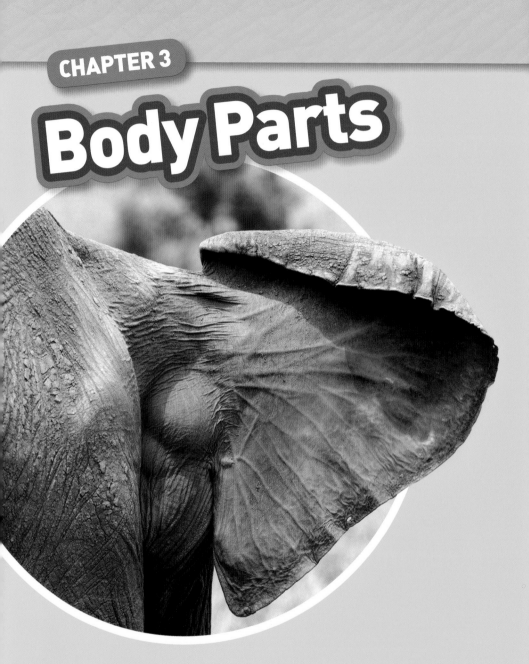

 Elephants use their big **ears** like fans to cool off when it's hot. They wave their ears to create a breeze.

 They also wave their **ears** at insects. Then the insects fly away.

YOU READ

When elephants sense danger, they hold out their ears to make themselves look bigger. This frightens their enemies.

Lions see the elephant's big ears. They are afraid. They run away.

Trunks are useful. They're like very long noses, but they can do much more than smell things. Elephants use them to scoop food and spray water into their mouths.

Elephants like to swim.
They use their **trunks** to
breathe while underwater.

Elephants also use their trunks to communicate in different ways. A mother wraps her trunk around her baby like a hug.

 Young elephants use their trunks to say hello. Then they play.

Asian elephant

African elephant

 YOU READ Elephants have **fingers** on the ends of their trunks. African elephants have two fingers, and they use them to grasp. Asian elephants have only one finger, and they use it to scoop.

Elephants pick up small leaves and fruit with their **fingers**.

YOUR TURN!

Look what an elephant does. How do you do these things?

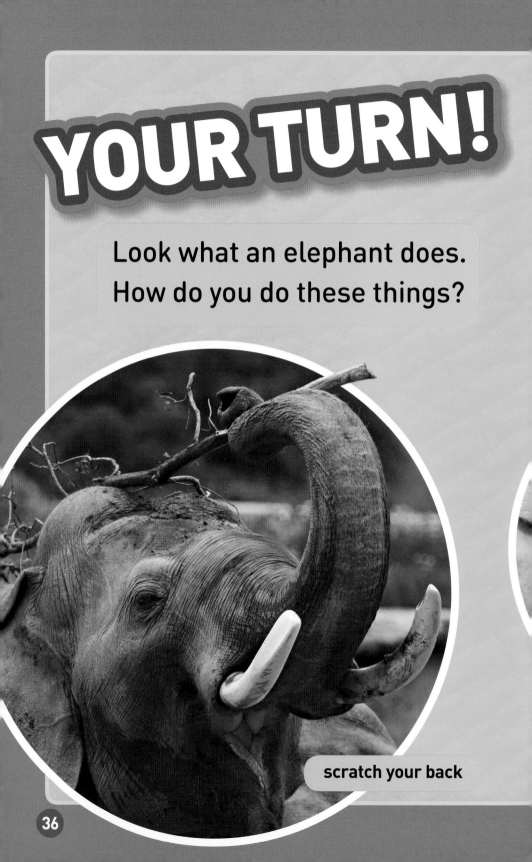

scratch your back

stay cool

eat

keep flies away

37

CHAPTER 4

What Elephants Need

YOU READ Since elephants are so large, they need to eat a lot. Hungry elephants spend many hours every day searching for **food**.

Elephants wake up early to find **food**. They can eat up to 18 hours each day.

Elephants are herbivores, which means they **eat** plants and not meat. They like to eat grass, leaves, and roots.

 Sometimes there isn't grass. Elephants pull down small trees. Then they can **eat** the leaves.

YOU READ Elephants need to **drink** a lot of water, too. Although the herd travels to find food, elephants remember where the water holes are.

The herd returns to the water. Here they **drink**, splash, and play.

YOUR TURN!

Elephants eat plants, not meat. Do you eat meat or plants or both? Tell which of these foods come from plants.

Where Elephants Live

There are approximately 470,000 African elephants in the wild, living in 37 countries south of the Sahara.

There are about 50,000 Asian elephants living in 13 countries throughout Asia. The elephant population has been in decline, but many organizations are working hard to help save them.

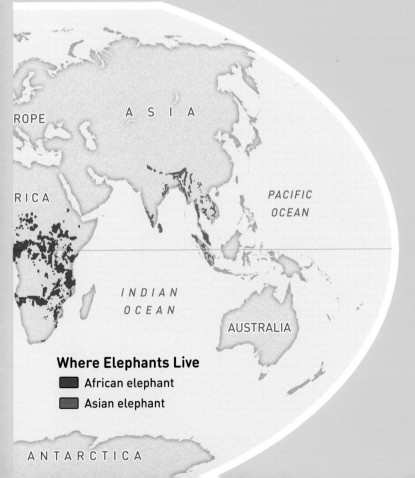

ROPE

A S I A

RICA

PACIFIC
OCEAN

INDIAN
OCEAN

AUSTRALIA

Where Elephants Live
African elephant
Asian elephant

ANTARCTICA

For Garth and Wil, whose love of science and nature
rekindled my own. —A. E. H.

Art Director: Amanda Larsen

The author and publisher gratefully acknowledge the expert literacy review of this book by Susan B. Neuman, Ph.D., professor of early childhood and literacy education, New York University.

Illustration Credits

COVER, Arco Images/Kimball Stock; Top border (throughout), happystock/Shutterstock;1 (CTR), Steve Bloom Images/Alamy; 3 (LO), Ariadne Van Zandbergen/Minden Pictures; 4 (LO), imageBROKER/Alamy; 5 (UP), Martin Withers/Minden Pictures; 5 (LO), Bildagentur Zoonar GmbH/Shutterstock; 6 (LE), Wacharachat Vaiyaboon/Alamy; 6-7 (CTR), Joe Austin/Minden Pictures; 8 (LE), Pradeep Soman/Alamy; 9 (RT), Bart Breet/Minden Pictures; 10 (LE), Frans Lanting/National Geographic Creative; 11 (CTR), Pete Oxford/Minden Pictures; 12 (LO), Sanchai Loongroong Photography/Getty Images; 15 (UP), Ian Wood/Alamy; 15 (LO), Nigel Pavitt/John Warburton-Lee Photography Ltd/Alamy; 16-17 (CTR), Anup Shah/Nature Picture Library; 18 (CTR), Wildlife Bildagentur/Kimball Stock; 19 (LO), Beverly Joubert/Getty Images; 20-21 (CTR), Steve Bloom/Getty Images; 22 (LE), Denis-Huot/Minden Pictures; 23 (UP), Jami Tarris/Corbis; 24 (UP LE), Suzi Eszterhas/Minden Pictures; 24 (UP RT), Cathy Hart/Design Pics/Getty Images; 24 (LO LE), Bart Breet/Minden Pictures; 24 (LO RT), Tim Fitzharris/Minden Pictures; 26 (CTR), Eric Baccega/Minden Pictures; 27 (UP), Andy Rouse/Minden Pictures; 28-29 (CTR), Gallo Images/Corbis; 30 (LO), Rob Crandall/Alamy; 31 (CTR), Marc Anderson/Alamy; 32 (CTR), Heinrch van den Berg/Getty Images; 33 (UP), Jeff Vanuga/Getty Images; 34 (CTR), ZSSD/Minden Pictures; 34 (UP), AfriPics.com/Alamy; 35 (RT), Denis-Huot Michel/Getty Images; 36 (CTR), Vladimir Wrangel/Shutterstock; 37 (UP), goldsaint/Getty Images; 37 (CTR LE), Theo Allofs/Minden Pictures; 37 (LO RT), Sergey Gorshkov/Getty Images; 38 (CTR), Gerry Ellis/Minden Pictures; 39 (CTR), Frans Lanting/National Geographic Creative; 40 (CTR), Hajarimanitra Rambeloarivony/Alamy; 41 (UP), Thomas Retterath/Getty Images; 42-43 (CTR), Winfried Wisniewski/Minden Pictures; 44 (CTR), nevodka/Shutterstock; 45 (UP), Nattika/Shutterstock; 45 (UP CTR), Shutterstock; 45 (LO CTR), Brilliance stock/Shutterstock; 45 (LO), Tim UR/Shutterstock; 47, NG Maps

Trade paperback ISBN: 978-1-4263-2618-9

Reinforced library binding ISBN: 978-1-4263-2619-6

National Geographic supports K–12 educators with ELA Common Core Resources. Visit natgeoed.org/commoncore for more information.

Printed in the United States of America
17/WOR/3